The Art of
MAKE ◆ DO
QUILTING

The Art of
MAKE  DO
QUILTING

MARY W. KERR

The Ultimate Guide for
Working with Vintage Textiles

SCHIFFER
PUBLISHING

4880 Lower Valley Road • Atglen, PA 19310

Other Schiffer Books on Related Subjects:

Portable Patchwork: The Women Pioneers of the Original Quick & Easy Quilting Method, with Projects for Today, Pamela Weeks, ISBN 978-0-7643-6202-6

Unconventional & Unexpected, 2nd Edition: American Quilts Below the Radar, 1950–2000, Roderick Kiracofe, ISBN 978-0-7643-6302-3

And Still We Rise: Race, Culture, and Visual Conversations, Carolyn L. Mazloomi, ISBN 978-0-7643-4928-7

Other Schiffer Books by the Author:

Southern Quilts: Celebrating Traditions, History, and Designs, ISBN 978-0-7643-5502-8

Recycled Hexie Quilts: Using Vintage Hexagons in Today's Quilts, ISBN 978-0-7643-4820-4

Twisted: Modern Quilts with a Vintage Twist, ISBN 978-0-7643-5170-9

Copyright © 2022 by Mary W. Kerr

Library of Congress Control Number: 2021942848

Cover and Interior design by Ashleey Millhouse

Type set in Mr Eaves Mod OT / Chronicle Text

ISBN: 978-0-7643-6313-9
Printed in India

Published by Schiffer Publishing, Ltd.
4880 Lower Valley Road
Atglen, PA 19310
Phone: (610) 593-1777; Fax: (610) 593-2002
Email: Info@schifferbooks.com
Web: www.schifferbooks.com

For our complete selection of fine books on this and related subjects, please visit our website at www.schifferbooks.com. You may also write for a free catalog.

Schiffer Publishing's titles are available at special discounts for bulk purchases for sales promotions or premiums. Special editions, including personalized covers, corporate imprints, and excerpts, can be created in large quantities for special needs. For more information, contact the publisher.

We are always looking for people to write books on new and related subjects. If you have an idea for a book, please contact us at proposals@schifferbooks.com.

To brave women everywhere who show up, stand tall and make it work.

You are my heart, my inspiration, and the hope for our future.

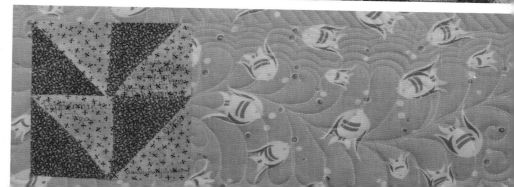

CONTENTS

INTRODUCTION

For as long as women have been quilting, we have been making things work. Our ability to adapt and readjust midstream reflects our unique determination and creativity. We make do with what is on hand. We finish projects left undone. We add to what was started and make it our own.

I have always been drawn to unfinished projects and abandoned blocks, tops and fragments. I love the challenge of incorporating these vintage pieces into my contemporary quilting. The idea of "recycling" these fabrics simply makes my heart sing! My mission has been to repurpose these fragments of yesterday into something that can be used and enjoyed for generations to come. I love the opportunity to combine blocks, attempt an innovative setting, or create a small quilt that showcases a limited number of blocks left to us from the past. Judging from the enthusiasm of my students around the world, I'm not the only one! Thousands of us truly love these aspects that form make-do quilting.

As I have worked with textiles over the years, I have found that some pieces are harder to reimagine than others. This book is about those pieces . . . the feed sacks, linens, vintage ephemera, old clothing, fragile textiles, and more. I wanted to explore the process of creating with some of these outsider pieces. How can we make them work? Can we use every imaginable scrap? What steps need to be taken to adapt to these challenges? How can we make them shine? How can we channel our make-do history into our contemporary work?

There are as many answers as there are vintage textiles. This book will give you many options to choose from, so that you can embrace all the joys of make-do quilting and learn the techniques for succeeding with challenging pieces that come your way.

The theme of make-do has been present during every era of our quilt-making history. If you run out of fabric, use something else. If you need an extra border, add one. If you are short on skills or talent, make it work. Use up those leftover blocks as you mix, match, and create.

This was not an "I don't care what you think" mentality but a mindset of making do. It allowed quilters of all socioeconomic levels to continue creating with whatever materials they had on hand.

This quirky attitude adds to the charm of our quilts. It's especially true in the older Southern pieces I have been fortunate enough to study and appreciate. I love the odd border, the use of a different block, and the often-unexpected pop of character!

Appreciating Pieces from the Past

My love of quilting began with an appreciation of historical textiles. I am honored to share a few favorite pieces from my collection. I invite you to study these quilts, note what makes your heart sing, and celebrate our history of make-do quilting. Women had choices, and we can learn volumes from their innovative decisions.

Blazing Star with Lamoy Star insets, circa 1870. This quilt came from a Texas estate and features a claret back.

Rising Sun top,
circa 1880, 58" ×
72", eastern
Tennessee

Detail of Rising
Sun top

Album and Stars top, circa 1870, 68″ × 68″

Maryland Star, circa 1840, 72″ × 73″.
Compton, Maryland.

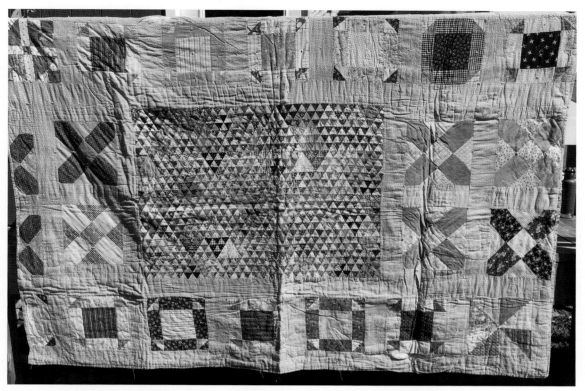

Tied Sampler, circa 1900, 72″ × 80″. This Georgia quilt is hand tied rather than quilted.

Make-Do Sampler top, circa 1890, 80″ × 88″

Double Sided Sampler quilt, circa 1890, 66″ × 68″, Illinois

Detail of Sampler quilt

Side B of Sampler quilt

Feathered Star, circa 1900, 82″ × 84″

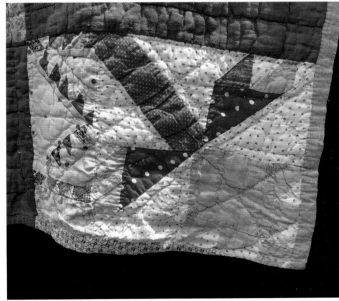

Feathered Star
make-do block

Oklahoma Sampler, circa 1920, 69″ × 80″. This tied quilt was thought to be made by Mary McCarty in Erik, Oklahoma. Mary and her husband, Henry, owned and operated a grocery on Old Route 66 in Erik.

Ducks Foot Sampler quilt, circa 1920, 64" × 68". The central unit
in this quilt is a Ducks Foot block from 1890. It is surrounded by
early-20th-century piecing. Provenance unknown.

Detail of Indigo
Star block

Indigo Star top,
circa 1900, 82″ ×
86″. This creative
maker used coping
strips around many
of the Star blocks to
allow for inconsis-
tencies in size.

Wonky Squares quilt, circa 1900, 62″ × 76″. This thick Southern
quilt features several sizes of squares and the signature Baptist
Fan or elbow quilting. Provenance unknown.

Indigo Sampler quilt, circa 1930, 66″ × 80″. Note the variety of pieced blocks that date from 1880 to 1930. No provenance known.

Nine Patch top, circa 1940, 60″ × 84″. Nine Patch squares from 1900 were bordered with pink in the 1940s.

Logs and Squares Sampler quilt, circa 1920, 55″ × 80″. This unknown quilt maker from North Georgia pieced her quilt by using a variety of blocks that span from 1880 to 1920.

Churn Dash quilt, circa 1930, 64″ × 84″. An unknown quilt maker in Wichita, Kansas, needed to use her creative piecing skills to make odd-sized blocks work.

Ocean Waves top, circa 1930, 68" × 80". This top was started in the 1980s and finished with an ice cream cone border in the 1930s. The peach fabric "almost" matches the cheddar.

Red Baskets Sampler top, circa 1940, 68" × 78". Note the wide variety of block size, scale, and placement.

Purple String quilt, circa 1940, 68" × 80". This thick Southern quilt is from North Alabama.

Basket and Butterflies quilt, circa 1940,
66″ × 75″. This unknown quilt maker from
East Texas surrounded her 1920s basket of
flowers with whimsical butterflies from
the 1940s.

Half Star, circa 1940, 54" × 72". One can only wonder if this quilt maker ran out of steam and made only half a star, or if she split her lone star in two. Provenance unknown.

Wedding Ring Make-Do, 1950, 66″ × 75″. This Pennsylvania quilter got creative with Wedding Ring units and chose to machine-stitch them to mint green rather than piece it traditionally.

Detail of Double
Wedding Ring

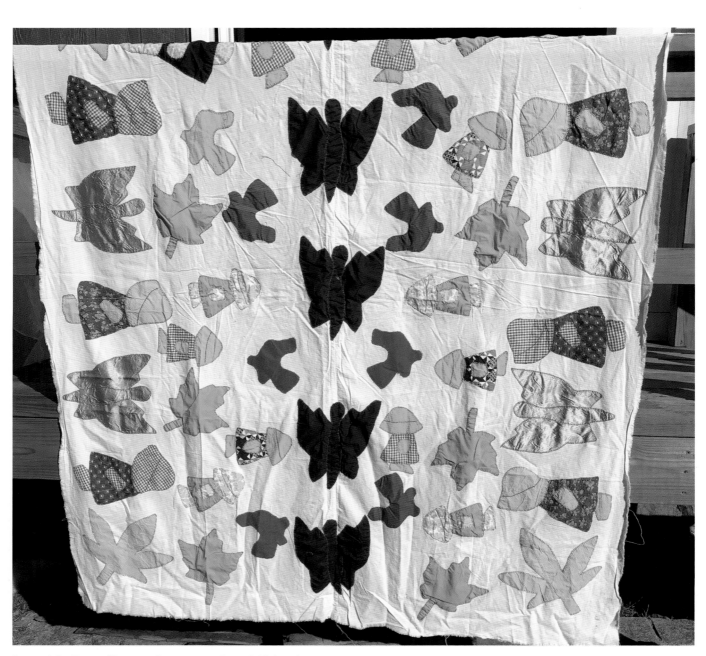

Sue and the Butterflies top, circa 1940, 66″ × 75″. This unknown quilt maker mastered the art of making do by using every fabric available. Who knew Sunbonnet Sues could be created out of gold lamé.

Nine Patch and Flying Geese Top, circa 1870, 82″ × 96″

CHAPTER 1

Making It Work with Vintage Blocks

Over the years there have been many projects left undone. Some quilts were never finished because of time constraints, others were not the quality of workmanship desired, and still others were victims of indecision, changing priorities or unavailable resources. (Sound familiar?) For whatever reason, we find an abundance of orphan blocks, works in progress, fragments, and tops. These are the pieces I want to give others permission to play with. These are the building blocks for your very own make-do quilt.

Fabrics, patterns, and eras can be mixed. Blocks can be added to or cut down. Pieces can be combined in new and unexpected ways. There are no "rules" . . . just a desire to make these textiles sing once again.

As I was creating pieces for this book, I chose to try and showcase multiple ways to use the same fabric or set of blocks. Most of the larger pieces I will share have smaller pieces created from the leftover bits. These scraps became mini quilts, pillows, pincushions and cracklin' mats (see page 161). In Southern cooking, the cracklings are those tasty bits left in the bottom of your pan. Tiny morsels that remind you how much you enjoyed your main meal.

Tip: Cracklin' mats use the tiniest leftover bits of fabric and are tangible
reminders of a great block, the perfect color combination, or
a favorite technique.

Cracklin' Mat,
5 1/2" × 5 1/2"

Shelter in Place,
36″ × 36″, machine-
quilted by Vicki
Maloney

Shelter in Place was created during the early months of the COVID-19 pandemic in 2020. I was isolating at home and found myself drawn to this black house block that had been gifted to me years ago from my buddy Pam Weeks. This quilt features vintage blocks, clothing, and fragments. The home is at the heart, but the sadness of the pandemic surrounds our sanctuary. The outer blocks are the Hands All Around pattern, representing how we all must come together to support and uplift each other. The bright Star blocks represent hope. The black fabrics used are mourning prints from the 1880s, which reflect the loss of life resulting from the pandemic.

Pathways, 43″ × 44″, machine-quilted by Dusty Farrell

Pathways was designed with longtime friend Dusty Farrell in mind. For years Dusty has teased that I hate him because **I so often send** him pink quilts to work on. I pulled fragments from seven different block sets that read black and indigo. The fabrics in this top were not as sturdy as we may have wished. Dusty heavily quilted the entire piece to hold those fragile fabrics in place beautifully. A fragment of another vintage top was used for the backing. If you look closely, you can see that I added only a sliver of pink to keep us both honest . . . and the cracklin' mat is pink.

Both *Four Square* and *Indigo Basket* were created using the same set of orphan Basket blocks pieced around 1900. *Four Square* uses four blocks in the center medallion with vintage pink and indigo fabrics and features an inner border pieced from extra orange and pink half squares that were part of the original Basket blocks. This square on point is surrounded by fragments from a Economy Block quilt top. The back was pieced using the rest of the blocks. *Indigo Baskets* features a single basket set with orphan Irish Chain blocks and fragments of a Trip Around the World top.

Four Square, 59″ × 59″, machine-quilted by Connie Stover

Indigo Basket, 40″ × 40″, machine-quilted by Diana Annis

Four floral appliqué blocks were used to create *Orange Is a Neutral*. These 1940s orange daisies were from a set of 11 blocks that were gifted to me from my dear friend Sue Reich. Eight blocks are incorporated into this quilt, and the remaining three are featured in *Daisy Chain* (seen on page 113). Four floral blocks were pieced to create a crossed center medallion, and the inner border used large brown hexagons from the 1970s. The outer border features daisy blocks that were cut down to form a funky petal design. Bright, bold, and beautiful!

Orange Is a Neutral, 35" × 35", machine-quilted by Jane Hauprich

Creamsicles in Chocolate, 44″ × 46″, hand- and machine-quilted by Allison Wilbur

Sunflower pillow, 15″ × 15″; pincushion with double buttons, 6″ × 6″; mini quilt 5″ × 7″; cracklin' mat, 4½″ × 6½″

Creamsicles in Chocolate was created when usable parts of five different vintage blocks and top fragments were combined. The 1870s cheddar petals were appliquéd to a thin gauzy fabric that was gently removed and reinforced with interfacing for support. I loved pairing the Dresden Plate blocks and flying geese strips with the cheddar ovals inserted in the border. Quilter Allison Wilbur added hand-quilted accents and vintage buttons for an unexpected pop.

Pair of cracklin'
mats, 4″ × 4″ each

Boys in the Garden,
42″ × 43″, machine-
quilted by MaryGin
and Michael
Rettman

Boys in the Garden combines a set of nine Overall Sam blocks with fragments of a damaged Grandmother's Flower Garden top. Hexagon blocks are fussy-cut to set with the boys and then bordered with fragments of that same top. I was careful to cut the border units so the paths were oriented in the same direction. The backing features fabric recycled from a floral dress of my grandmother's.

For *Fruit Loops*, poorly made circular blocks were reconstructed so they could lie flat. The center circle in a square block is the only one that was completed when these blocks were first pieced in the 1940s. The remaining circles were dome shaped and hard to work with. My solution was to trim them into squares and set with vintage fabric. This scrap of Bubblegum Pink fabric was damaged, and yet we were able to make it work. The center unit was bordered with a fragment of a Bow Tie top. When I purchased the top at a yard sale, someone had inked "$1" directly onto the fabric. The placement of the colors and the movement of the blocks is so much fun. The before-quilting image is adorable, but once Kelly Cline added her stitches, this piece is magical.

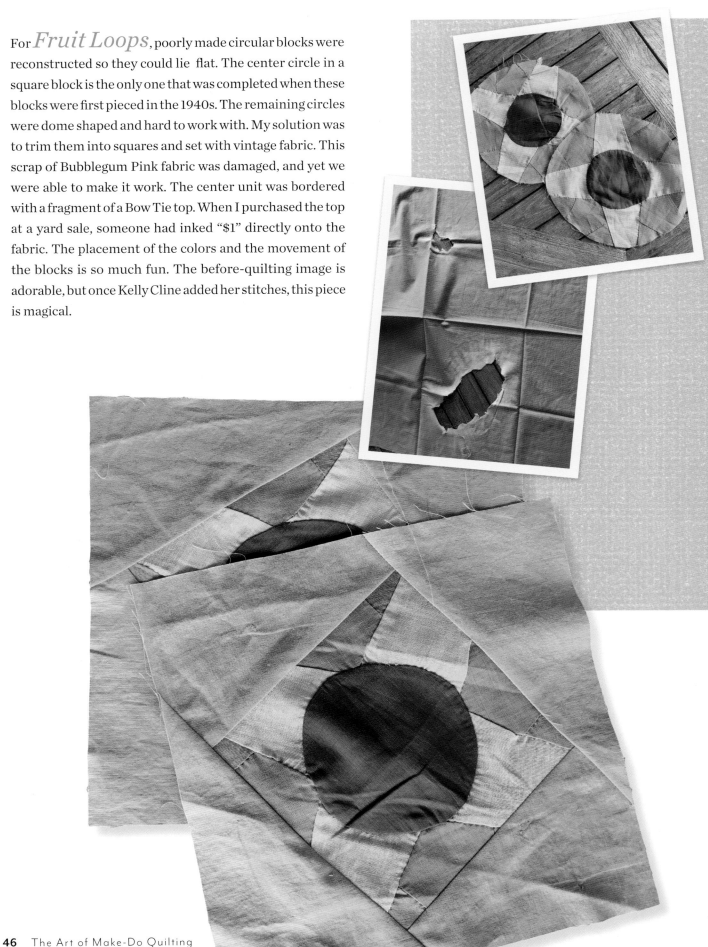

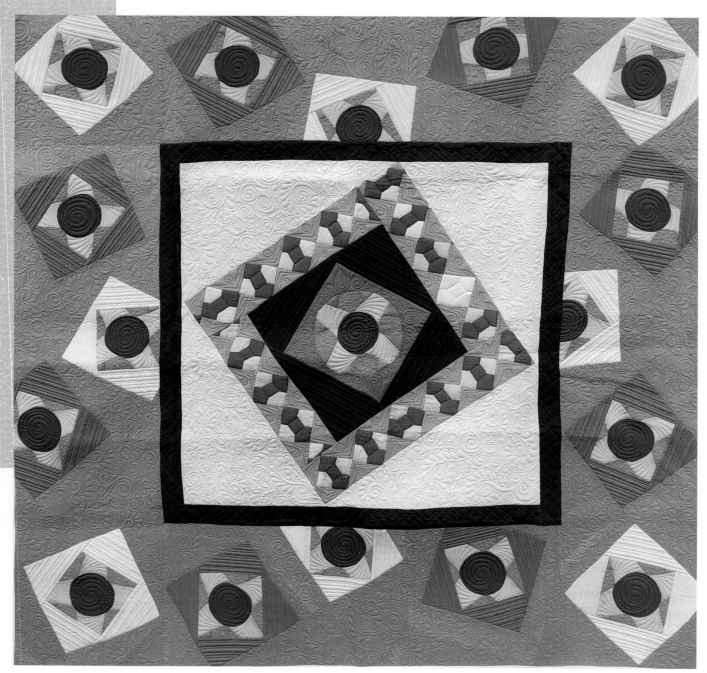

Fruit Loops, 56" × 60", machine-quilted by Kelly Cline

Baskets of Chicken grew organically as I added border after border to this lonely little Chicken block that was left over from another project. My buddy Kris Vierra had given me a set of partial Basket blocks to play with. These cheery yellow basket bases were missing their handles. I loved the opportunity to place them in a new and exciting way. The random-squares top had been basted over a feed sack. Once I unstitched the top from the backing, I was able to use the top for the borders and corner-setting pieces. I ran short on fabric, so the outer corners are heavily pieced to use every scrap. A true make-do moment!

Basket of Chicken, 62″ × 62″, machine-quilted by Kris Vierra

Pincushion, 3½″ × 3½″; cracklin' mats, 6½″ and 5¼″ square

Social Isolation, 36½″ × 37″, machine-quilted by Cheryl Morgan

Social Isolation features a house block from 1900 surrounded by vintage fabrics and two block fragments from the same era. I wanted to reflect the simplicity and struggle of our family's situation during the COVID pandemic. We insulated ourselves in our homes while worrying about the world outside our doors. We missed our children, friends, hugs, and favorite hiking trails. The realization that this pandemic was not ending soon was sobering and sad. I used a vintage top fragment for the back.

CHAPTER 2

Mix It Up, Make It Work:
Quilting with Vintage Linens

Many of my students enjoy the challenge of working with textiles that are different colors, patterns, and designs. Bringing pieces together that started their lives in two or more different homes by multiple makers just makes us smile. The result is a happy collaboration with lots of trial and error and the spirit of making do.

All the quilts in this chapter incorporate vintage linens and embroidery. I generally work from the center of the quilt and allow myself to add borders until it tells me to stop. I do not work from a preset plan, and I often change design decisions as I work.

Choose your vintage linen and see what other textiles seem to coordinate. Do you have a set of blocks with similar colors? Maybe you find a fabric that enhances the design, or vintage trim that might play well. Gather more than you think you will need, and allow yourself to edit as you go.

Hint: Play with placement and use your digital camera to take pictures of the process. This gives a point of reference to return to and lets one rearrange pieces without the fear of "forgetting" our favorite arrangement.

Mary's Garden was created using a vintage tea towel embroidered with my initials, M.K., and a pair of festive carrots. I chose to add the bright Compass block to complement the orange carrots and the embroidered Sunray blocks to gently border the center. These outer blocks were cut in half and arranged to create a frame.

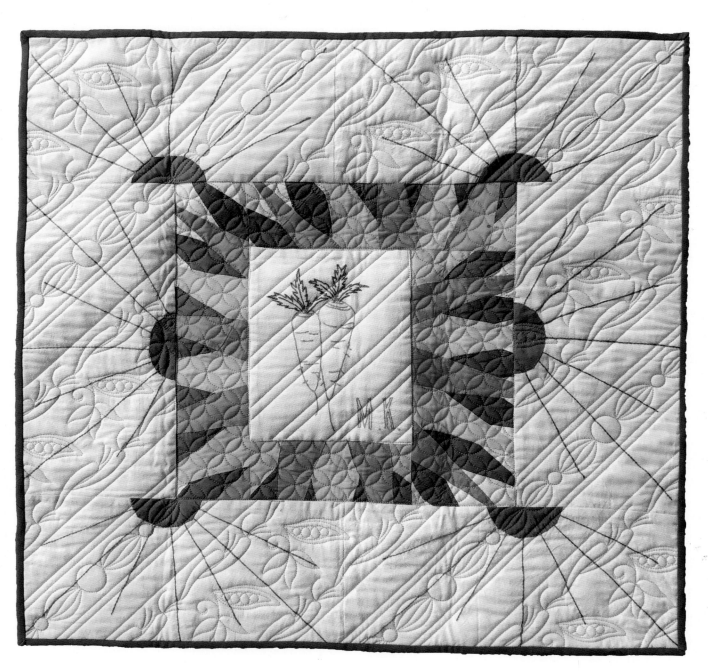

Mary's Garden, 23″ × 23″, machine-quilted by Cheryl Morgan

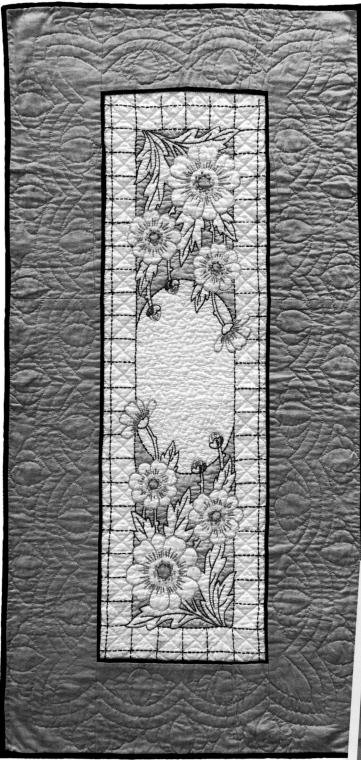

Blue Flowers for Karen was inspired by a dresser scarf that was embroidered by my great-grandmother Crissie Say (1883–1969) in the 1930s. I chose not to cut apart the textile. It was stained, but I wanted to keep it whole. This floral embroidery was paired with a linen jacket and backed with fabric from the 1950s. I used a black flange to frame the delicate blue flowers.

Blue Flowers for Karen, 24″ × 60″, hand-quilted by Doris Bloomer

Hint: A flange is a great way to add a pop of color to a piece and separate the units. One-inch strips are folded in half and inserted into the seam. Sew the raw edges of the folded fabric along the seam line and then piece as normal. To hide the stitches, move your needle on your machine one step to the left.

Hint: Both Restoration and Retro Clean are excellent products to brighten up yellowed blocks and remove stains.

An Apple a Day was created when I was playing with pieces from an appliqué quilt that was falling apart. Many pieces were missing, but I was able to salvage four of the red basket bases and pair them with this adorable dog and his apple embroidery block. It was a single lonely orphan block that now has a new family of 1940s baskets and an 1880s Mosaic border.

Mother and Child, 22″ × 26″, machine-quilted by Mary Kerr

Mother and Child started as an unfinished embroidery that had been twisted out of square. I chose to embrace the inconsistencies and pair it with poorly made 25-Patch blocks that were taken apart and resewn to create a border that waves as well.

The House on Claret Mountain was created when I challenged myself to use a dresser scarf in multiple ways. Half of the scarf was bordered by vintage claret fabric and Ducks Feet blocks. Claret is a burgundy dye that was extremely popular from 1885 to 1910. The other half of the dresser scarf was cut apart and used to create five smaller pieces . . . a mini quilt, three cracklin' mats, and a pincushion.

Mini quilts 4½″ × 5″ to 8″ × 8″; pincushion 3½″ × 4″

The House on Claret Mountain, 19½″ × 24″, machine-quilted by Diana Beverage

Ready to Roll features a Vogart pillow top that was paired with Mosaic fragments from the 1890s. This WWII soldier motif was a popular motif during the war years. This same top was used in *Social Isolation,* as seen on page 51.

Toy Soldier, 8″ × 8″

Ready to Roll, 26″ × 25″, machine-quilted by Januari Rhodes

Peppermint Tea,
26″ × 26″, machine-
quilted by Deb
Peterson

Peppermint Tea was inspired by a worn table-cloth with cheery teapots in the four corners. I loved the combination of appliqué with embroidery and chose to use all of these teapots in one piece. The linen was reinforced with interfacing, and the teapots were rejoined to form a four-block center medallion. This was bordered with fragments of a 1900s Pinwheel Top that had its own make-do history. Check out that one oops block! Vintage red rickrack was inserted in between the center and the border for an unexpected pop of color and texture. A vintage feed sack was used for the back.

Cracklin' mats,
4¼" × 5¾" and
4¾" × 4¾"

What's Cookin'? features a kitchen towel that was cut down to remove the damaged edge and then bordered with fragments of a Nine-Patch top that had seen better days. Seams were popping and fabric was missing, but I was able to cut around the damage to make it work. The cracklin' mats created used leftover scraps both from *What's Cookin'?* and *Neighbors* on page 123.

What's Cookin?, 19¹⁄₂″ × 22″, machine-quilted by Diana Beverage

No Place Like Home, 39" × 36", machine-quilted by
Cheryl Morgan

Both *No Place Like Home* and *Bicycle Built for Two* were created when I layered a vintage embroidery on top of a quilt top fragment. This allows the design to flow, since we are not cutting borders and worrying about corners matching.

I wanted to incorporate the crocheted edging in *No Place Like Home,* so the linen was stitched to the top and then quilted as a whole. In *Bicycle Built for Two* I had Cheryl Morgan quilt the base first and then we appliquéd the tea towel onto the quilted piece and added more stitches. Two different ways to make it work!

Bicycle Built for Two, 22″ × 21″, machine-quilted by Cheryl Morgan

God Bless Our Home, 19″ × 16½″, machine-quilted by Vicki Maloney

God Bless Our Home was an opportunity to use multiple orphan blocks with a sentimental embroidered sampler. I had one T block from the 1860s and Four Star blocks from 1890. These were cut apart to create a framed border that works perfectly with the 1940s embroidery. Do not be afraid to use partial blocks!

Hummingbird Kisses was created when I wanted to play with this funky appliqué and embroidered block. I loved this single orphan with its oversized water lily and tiny butterflies. How could you not smile at something whose scale was so unique? I added two borders to complete the quilt . . . Penny Square fragments from the 1930s and a 1920s Snowball top. I kept the outside simple so the Water Lily block would be my focus. Lynn O'Neal added the quilted hummingbird to perfectly complete the composition.

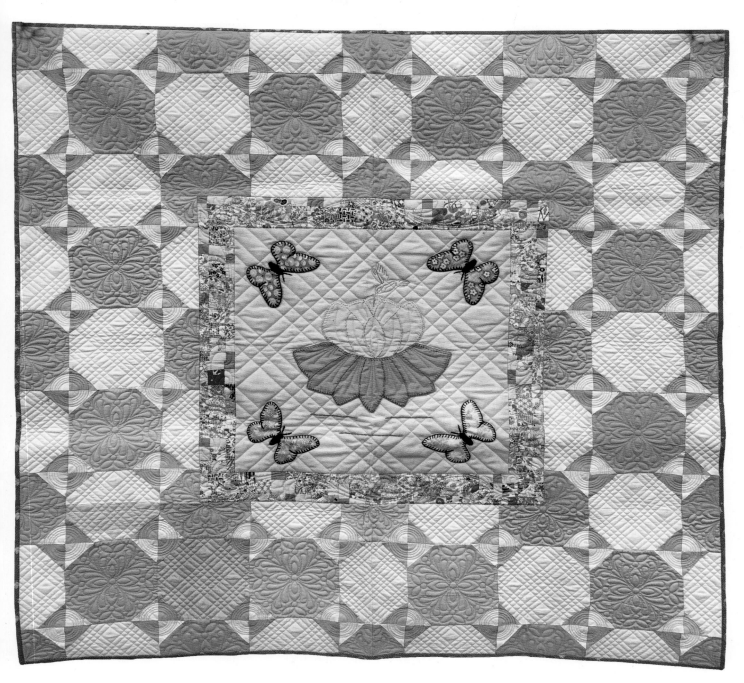

Hummingbird Kisses, 42″ × 42″, machine-quilted by Lynn O'Neal

CHAPTER 3

Unexpected Endings

When working with textiles that were started in one generation and are now being finished in ours, we often struggle with the thought that we are altering another woman's design. We can imagine what the maker envisioned; as a result, we are presented with two options. We can finish the piece as the maker intended, or we can choose to have an unexpected ending. As make-do quilters we have the choice to go either direction.

Minnie Opal Wilson (1912–2007)

My grandmother Opal Wilson was known for her needle skills, her willingness to try every craft technique ever invented, her determination, and her prolific quilting. It is estimated that she worked on over 300 quilts in her lifetime. She pieced quilts, hand-quilted them, and quilted for others in her Kansas home. I was the only one of her grandchildren who quilted. As a result, I became the recipient of most of her unfinished projects. This chapter shares a few of the ways I was able to incorporate her unfinished work into cherished memory pieces.

In the 1950s, our grandmother worked at the Nat Nast Bowling Shirt factory in Bonner Springs, Kansas. She could bring home the castoffs, and many of these scraps found their way into her quilts. This green-and-white top was one of her unfinished pieces. For *Opal's Garden*, I removed rows to square it up and kept this lap quilt as large as possible. *Sunflowers and Spiderwebs* was created with the leftover blocks. I took her blocks apart and resewed them into circles. I embraced her free-spirit quilting and her disdain for precision piecing. She used every imaginable white fabric, and some simply melted as I tried to iron them flat!

Opal's Garden, 53″ × 68″, machine-quilted by Jill Coleman

Sunflowers and Spiderwebs, 36″ × 36″, machine-quilted by Jill Coleman

Sunflowers and Spiderwebs, detail

Opal's Garden, detail

A stack of Tiffany blue stars had been pieced in the 1980s. They had never been finished, refused to lie flat, and were a challenge to work with. Thank you, Grandma Opal! I released the blocks from their side-setting pieces and paired them with vintage blocks, an embroidered piece, and a tattered apron. *Morgan Say*, *Katherine Elizabeth*, and *Samantha Corene* are named after three of Opal's great-granddaughters.

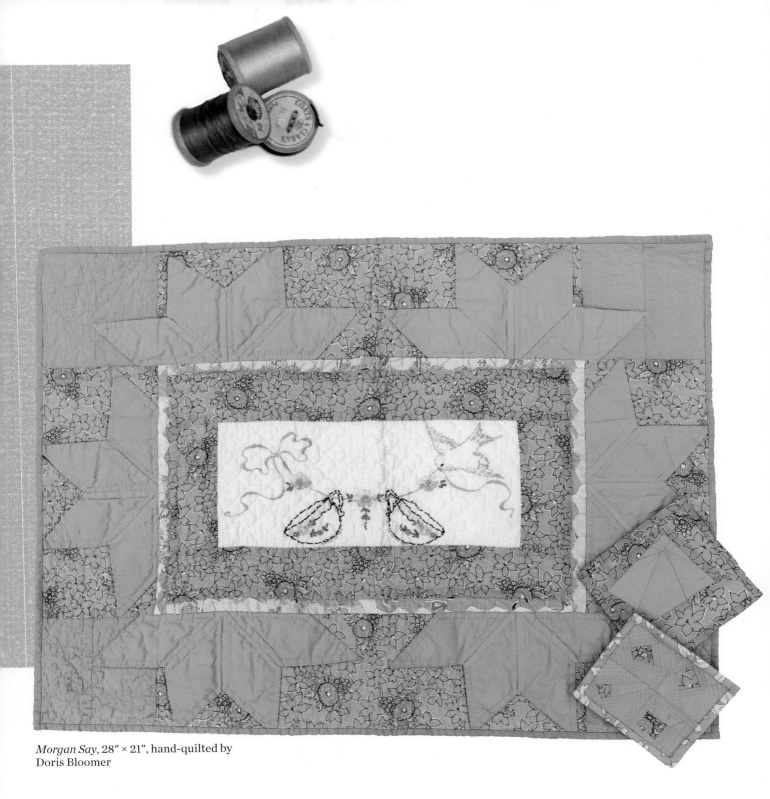

Morgan Say, 28″ × 21″, hand-quilted by
Doris Bloomer

Katherine Elizabeth, 20″ × 20″, machine-quilted by Allison Wilbur

Samantha Corene, 17″ × 17″, machine-quilted by Allison Wilbur

This tumbling-block top was missing three blocks from the top row. Rather than remaking the blocks with another fabric, I chose to remove the rest of that row and have this finished as Grandma pieced it. Only after it was quilted did I notice the placement errors and inconsistency of pattern. She may have gotten frustrated and put it aside to be fixed later. I love it just like it is, and I call it *The Stars Have Tumbled*.

The leftover blocks were paired with the embroidery from one of a set of pillowcases Opal had embroidered. *Flowers on My Pillow* used up almost every remaining scrap of these blue and tan fabrics.

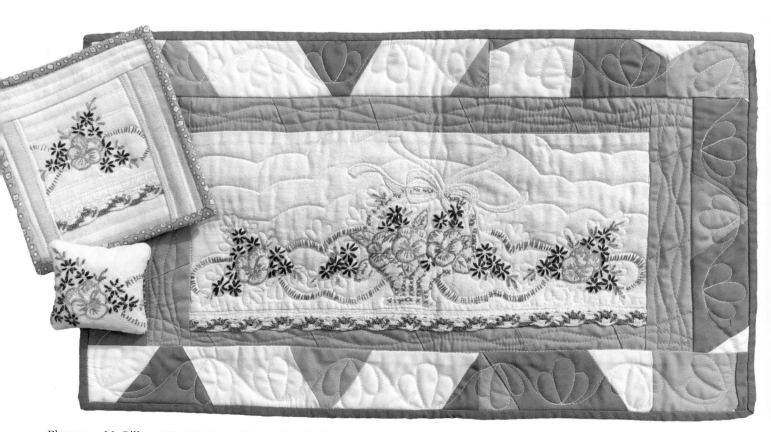

Flowers on My Pillow, 20″ × 11½″, machine-quilted by Shannon Shirley

The Stars Have Tumbled, 64″ × 77″, pieced by Opal Wilson in 1980, machine-quilted by Cheryl Morgan in 2019

Pink Flowers Everywhere, 24″ × 24″, machine-quilted by Diana Beverage

Pink Flowers Everywhere was created to use the remaining pillowcase embroidery. I bordered this fragment with two different vintage tops. The tan one was purchased for $1, and the pink squares were also used in *Bottoms Up*, as seen on page 135.

The final set of Opal's blocks was the Carpenter's Wheel pattern in green and white. None of the stars would lie flat, and the wonkiness of this piecing just made me smile. Opal quilted into her 90s, using what she had in the way she was most comfortable. I was and continue to be inspired by her make-do attitude.

Opal Wilson, 1995

Cracklin' mats, 4" × 4" to 6½" × 7"

CHAPTER 4

100 LBS. NET

MURRAY'S

BROILER FEED

MURRAY'S HATCHERY

Feed Sack Frenzy

Throughout history, many of our dry goods were delivered in fabric bags called feed sacks. If it could not be grown in a garden—flour, sugar, coffee, rice, chicken feed, fertilizer—it was purchased at the nearest general store. Fortunately for quilt lovers, these staple items were packed in cotton bags that, in the hands of resourceful women, not only became clothing and household items for their families but found their way into quilts. These unbleached cotton bags could be imprinted with a customer's logo, using permanent dye. Removing the dye was a labor-intensive job for the women who wanted to remove the printing and use the fabric.

I love finding a feed sack used in a vintage quilt. The ingenuity of the quilters who came before me is apparent in their willingness to make do and use what they had. We occasionally find bags that were not bleached and repurposed. These leftover treasures are now finding their way into my new quilts as backings and interesting pops of texture. What if you tried some of these ideas on your next projects? Take a look at this chapter's situations and which options I chose for making do, and see what techniques might be right for your stack of pieces.

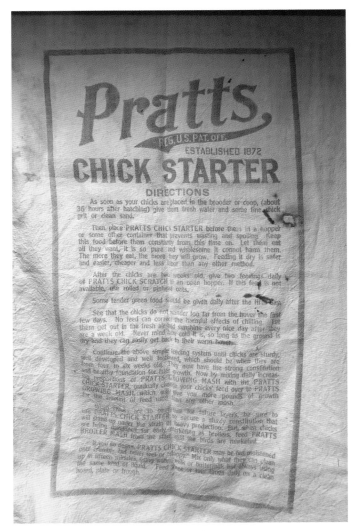

Back of Pratt Food Company feed sack

Pratt Food Company feed sack

Detail of feed sack Basket top

Sunfed feed sack top, circa 1940, 58″ × 72″

Feed sack Basket top, circa 1940, 62″ × 70″

Shenandoah Spring was designed around a vintage towel that had been painted using TriChem paints in the 1950s. It was bordered with vintage fabric from the 1880s and a coarse, uniquely pieced, Hexagon quilt top from the 1960s. The white fabrics used in this top were also feed sacks, and the holes where they were sewn together with thick thread are still visible. I used a vintage feed sack on the back that once held grass seed from the Queen Turf company in Bound Brook, New Jersey.

Shenandoah Spring, 22″ × 28″, machine-quilted by Shannon Shirley

Pincushion, 5″ × 5″

Mini quilt, 8″ × 8″, and cracklin' mats, 5″ × 5″
and 5½″ × 7½″

A strip of seven Redwork blocks begged to be made into something! *Murray's Barnyard* was created when I sashed six of the blocks with a vintage top fragment from 1900. The sashing strips were fussy-cut so that all the squares were oriented in the same direction. I wanted to make sure this gaggle of barnyard animals was the focus of the quilt. A feed sack from Murray's Broiler Feed in Ocean View, Delaware, was used on the back. The remaining Redwork block and top scraps were made into a mini quilt, cracklin' mats, and a pincushion.

Murray's Barnyard, 29½" × 34", machine-quilted by Michael and MaryGin Rettman

Looking West, 29″ × 30″, machine-quilted by Diana Beverage

Looking West features a Vogart pillow top of an Indian maiden that has been bordered with fragments of a 1900 Mosaic top and vintage flannel. The colors in the hexagon pieces pair beautifully with the tinted artwork and bright embroideries in this pillow top. This piece is backed with a feed sack from Roller Mills Flour in Grand Island, Nebraska.

Lawrence was created to showcase this feed sack that was found in a box of my grandmother's things. She had used the unprinted side of the feed sack to stitch an embroidered Mamma Bunny going shopping. The feed sack is from Zephyr Mills in Lawrence, Kansas, the largest town near her home in Linwood. My father remembers this mill in operation and recalls shopping there for flour. The other side of the quilt features a single Indigo orphan block bordered by two different square top fragments. One of these tops was also used in *Indigo Basket*, as seen on page 39.

Lawrence, 36″ × 36″, machine-quilted by Cheryl Morgan

Crazy quilt, circa 1900

Trade Mark, 27″ × 27″, machine-quilted by Cheryl Morgan

Feed sacks were used as the base of this turn-of-the-20th-century Crazy Quilt. The piece had never been finished, and the front fabrics were damaged beyond repair. I was fascinated by the black, red, and white printing on the back and the maker's creative use of available fabrics. These feed sacks came from Clarks Fertilizer in New York City. I repurposed these fragments into *Trade Mark* and left the decorative stitching in place. Vintage flannel was used as the border and the backing.

Shot Bag Quilts Several years ago, my cousin Victor contacted me and asked if I could create quilts out of buckshot bags (yes, he thinks I can do anything!). He had been at an auction and purchased five bags that once held hard lead shot. These had belonged to his sister-in-law's father, and he wanted to create memory pieces for her. These bags were small and heavier than most feed sacks. Several were marked with ink and stained. I was challenged to reinforce the surrounding fabrics so these pieces could lie flat. Vicki Maloney worked with me to quilt these pieces densely, so the discrepancies in fabric densities were not apparent. Together we were able to create four quilts and a pillow by adding vintage red, white, and blue top fragments. A memory label was added to the back of each quilt.

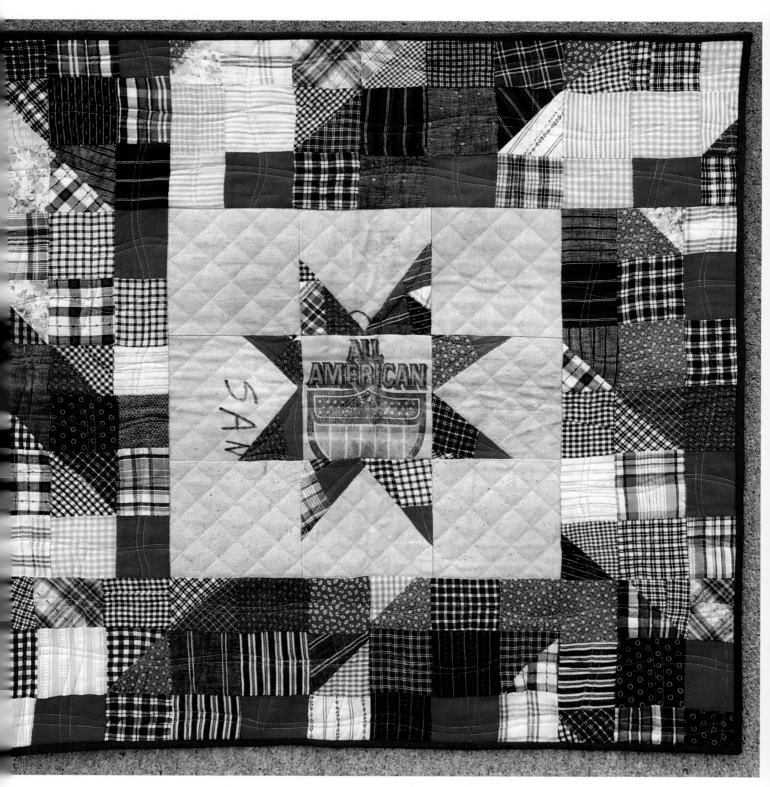

Shot Bag Quilt #4, 18″ × 18″, machine-quilted by Vicki Maloney

Shot Bag Quilt #1, 26″ × 18″, machine-quilted by Vicki Maloney

Shot Bag Pillow, 14″ × 14″, machine-quilted by Mary Kerr

Shot Bag Quilt #3, 24″ × 24″, machine-quilted by Vicki Maloney

Shot Bag Quilt #2, 24″ × 24″, machine-quilted by Vicki Maloney

Shortly after I finished the *Shot Bag* quilts, I found this thin bag from Kerr Salt Company, located in Philadelphia and Baltimore. I used it as the centerpiece for *Heart of Our Home*. The thin bag was envelope-finished to stabilize the fabric and then appliquéd onto the house block in the center of this quilt. This central unit was bordered with three block sets I had used in other quilts. The Hands All Around blocks were featured in *Social Isolation* (see page 51), the Flying Geese units in *Pathways* (see page 36), and the Mosaic top in *Looking West* (see page 99).

Heart of Our Home, 29" × 30", machine-quilted by Mo Starkey

CHAPTER 5

Who Would Have Thought We Could Use That?

Orange Petals pillow, 8″ × 8″

Sometimes we find fabric items that just do not fit into the traditional sandbox for quilt fabrics. What if an item is not 100% cotton? What if the fabric is too thick? Too flimsy? How can we make it work?

As I have shared before, my grandma Opal loved her TriChem paints. She frequently made these painted faces into potholders for use in her kitchen. I had one lonely orange face left, and chose to pair it with leftovers from *Orange Is a Neutral* (see page 41), to create *Daisy Chain*. Who says you can't have potholders on your quilt? Leftover petals were made into this sweet pillow that features a vintage button.

Daisy Chain, 23" × 26", machine-quilted by Cheryl Morgan

A Rose in the Kitchen, 16″ × 16″, machine-quilted by Mary Kerr

This crocheted potholder was made in the 1950s by an unknown relative. Many of my great-aunts shared patterns, and I remember all of them working on similar pieces. *A Rose in the Kitchen* was created when a single potholder was stitched onto a block from the 1940s. I quilted the vintage block first and then machine appliquéd the crocheted piece in place.

Alley Cats, 27″ × 22″, machine-quilted by Cheryl Morgan

Alley Cats was a pillow in its former life. The teal satin fabric behind the cats was slippery and was not interested in playing nicely with a cotton border. I chose to release the cats from their pillow back and trim this front unit as small as possible. The Star blocks were set with vintage mourning print fabric and pieced to create a border. I loved adding the one orange block for a pop of color.

Buckles, 27″ × 27″, machine-quilted by Vicki Maloney

Cracklin' mats, 4″ and 6½″ square

These next three quilts were created when I was experimenting with fragile fabrics. Could I make it work using textiles that were literally falling apart? The answer is sometimes, and it may be more work than you are willing to devote. All three of these started with pale embroidered animal blocks. I pieced these mini tops, and then my talented friend Shannon Shirley added InkTense pencils to brighten up the colors and make these critters pop.

Buckles is an adorable squirrel that was paired with two vintage blocks from the 1870s and a top fragment that had been heavily mended. Vicki Maloney worked with me to densely quilt this one with strategic stitches to hold everything in place.

Jo-Jo the Goat, 22″ × 22″, machine-quilted by Vicki Maloney

The fabrics for *Jo-Jo the Goat* were recycled from a cutter quilt fragment. I unquilted the original textile so that I could reuse the Monkey Wrench blocks and the homespun back. This is a time-consuming process that demands patience and a good seam ripper.

Cracklin' mat, 4″ × 4″

When creating *Horace the Horse*, I challenged myself to use a vintage chicken-scratch apron and a top fragment with damaged silk pieces. I cut around the damage and was able to create multiple borders, using these two textiles and the homespun fabric used in *Jo-Jo the Goat*.

Cracklin' mat, 8" × 8"

Horace the Horse, 31½″ × 28″, machine-quilted by Vicki Maloney

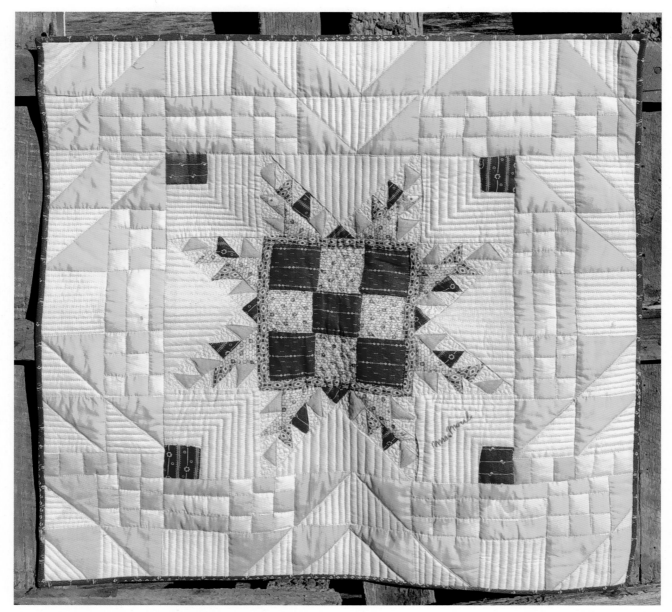

Neighbors, 25″ × 25″, machine-quilted by Diana Beverage

Hint: Feel free to mix and match fabrics from different eras. Complementary colors can be found that span generations.

What do you do when you have only two blocks? These were from different makers in two different eras. One was signed by Mrs. Moul in the 1920s, and the other was a stained block from the Say side of my family from the 1940s. My grandmother Katherine Elizabeth Pickering Say (1912–2003) was a lifetime quilter and an accomplished needlewoman. She loved many things, including her grandchildren, a mean game of cards, her gardens, and trading signed quilt blocks with her sisters and friends. She and Mrs. Moul could have easily been *Neighbors*.

Turtle pillow, 12″ × 12″

Deep in a box of things, I found this crocheted turtle that was probably made by one of my great-grandmothers in the 1940s. These turtles were crocheted around a bar of soap and kept near the sink to be used in the home. I stitched this memory piece to a cutter quilt fragment and made this small *Turtle Pillow*.

Mom Is Feeling Grinchy, 6" × 7", machine-quilted by Mary Kerr

A sweatshirt on a quilt? Who would have ever thought that would be possible? *Mom Is Feeling Grinchy* was created when I wanted to save a fragment of a favorite sweatshirt that I wore for years. The embroidered placket was bordered with block fragments and vintage red from the 1890s.

Memory quilts for men are not always easy. When my father-in-law, Thomas Kerr (1927–2020), passed away, I struggled to make something for my husband that would honor his dad. I took one of his ties that featured the Kerr family crest, and created this small wall hanging, *Remembering*, for my husband's office. The polyester fabric is not easy to piece with, so I recommend a simple pattern and patience.

Remembering, 14″ × 14″, machine-quilted by Marsha Swanson

Bambie, 3″ × 4″, cross-stitch created in 1990s, machine-quilted by Mary Kerr

Both *Bambie* and *Santa* were created using cross-stitch pieces that were created in the 1980s. Bambie was found on a small pillow, and the Santa image was stitched by my husband's aunt Arline Hennighan (1931–2011). These are not our normal quilting materials, but they can easily be incorporated into these memory pieces.

Cracklin' mats, 3½″ × 4½″ each, and pincushion, 2″ × 3″

Santa, 9″ × 9½″, cross-stitch created in
1982, machine-quilted by Mary Kerr

What about crocheted pieces? Can we make them work in a quilt? Absolutely! Vintage doilies, a cutter quilt back, and lots of buttons were used to create *62 Pansies*. The crocheted doilies and vintage rick rack were stitched directly onto the cutter quilt base by using my domestic machine. Use an open-toe foot and move slowly. Your machine thread is thinner than the crochet thread, so your stitches can be hidden as you secure the doily to your base. Vintage buttons from both grandmothers were used to secure the edges of the 62 pansies.

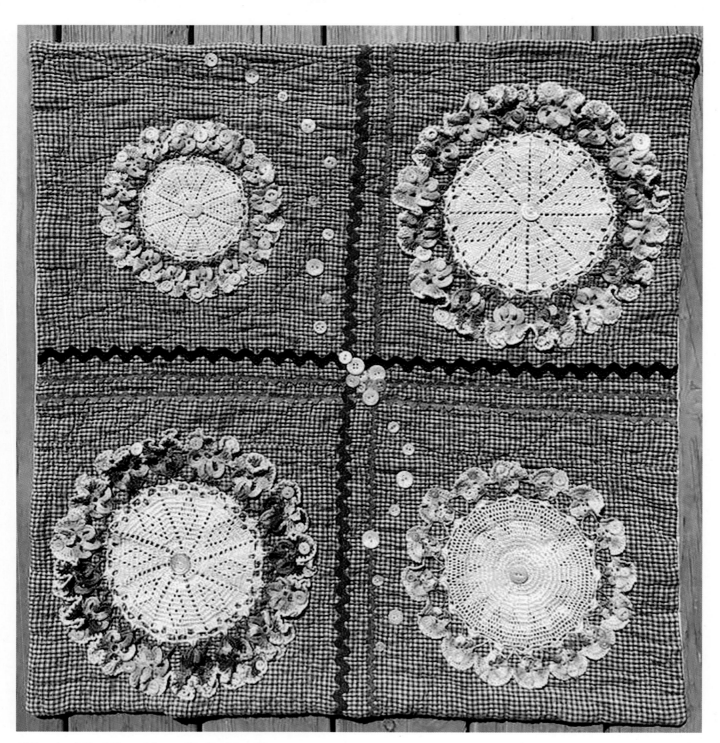

62 Pansies, 36" × 36", machine-quilted by Mary Kerr

Temperance, 37″ × 37″, machine-quilted by Vicki Maloney

Temperance What about vintage needlepoint? What steps need to be taken to make this fit into a quilt? I was gifted this floral needlepoint that was created in the 1970s and struggled with the weight and thickness of the textile. I first had to block the needlepoint to make it square (thank you, YouTube). I then paired it with Star blocks from the 1880s and three different vintage tops. Extra batting was added under the pieced blocks to even out the thickness of the quilt. I used a fun vintage flannel on the back. Gotta love that price!

Hint: Be adventurous with your backing fabrics. I love the surprise of a novelty print or the visual interest of a vintage textile, top, or fragment. Backings are a great way to recycle clothing, use older fabrics in your stash, and celebrate the unusual.

Cracklin' mat, 5″ × 8″

Bottoms Up was a sheet in its former life. My grandmother painted this sheet in the 1950s, and it was well loved. I saved the painted baby on the corner and surrounded her with fragments of a pink-and-white square top from the 1920s. The asymmetrical placement and the edition of a narrow framed border adds visual interest. Vintage rickrack was inserted in the binding to add an extra pop of texture and color.

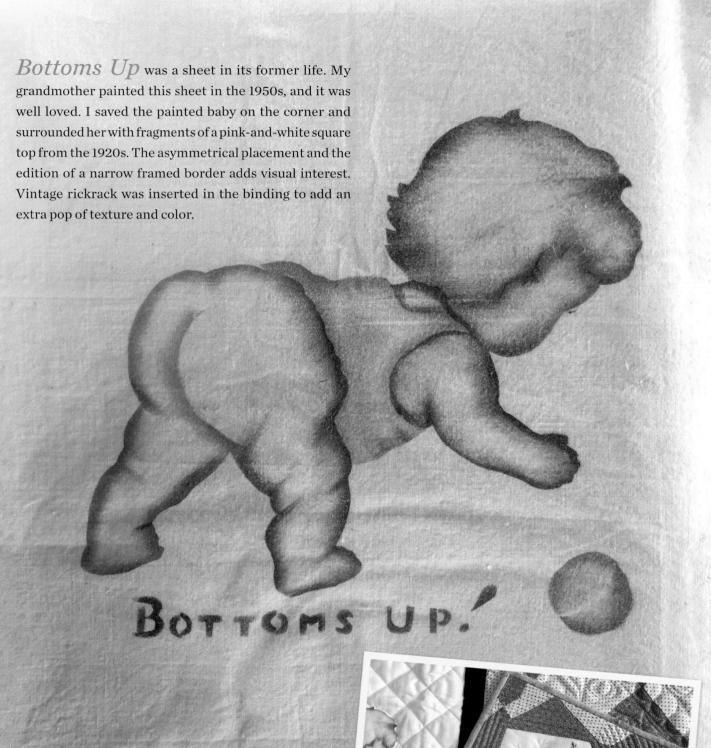

Pink Flowers mini quilt, 9½" × 10", and a pincushion, 3½" × 4½"

Bottoms Up, 27″ × 27″, machine-quilted by
Lucinda Herring

Georgia on My Mind, 36″ × 36″, machine-quilted by Cheryl Morgan

Georgia on My Mind is a memory piece that will be treasured for years to come. I am from Athens, Georgia, and all of these elements remind me of home. This heavy money bag originally came from a local bank in town and was found in my father-in-law's workshop. The Jacob's Ladder blocks were purchased at a meeting of the Atlanta Quilt Study Group. They had been cut out of a top, and the extra fabric had to be carefully removed. The backing is a Tugalo River feed sack from Lavonia Roller Mills in Lavonia, Georgia, a small town near Athens. All these elements were happily combined with a make-do mindset. If the pieces are important, the quilt will be perfect despite its imperfections.

Please Return To

The Citizens & Southern National Bank
Athens, Georgia

$1,000

CHAPTER 6

Use It Up: Celebrating Small

As I worked on pieces for this book, I found myself looking for ways to use up the smallest scraps of vintage fabric. Some quilts just asked to be smaller pieces, and tiny memory quilts were created. I found this was a perfect way to practice new techniques, and a great way to spread the wealth if you want to share a special textile with multiple family members.

The penny square for *Moo!* was once part of this damaged baby quilt. I salvaged the blocks, soaked them in RetroClean, and then incorporated some of them into small quilts. This small size also gives me the opportunity to use scraps of fabrics for the backings and dig into my leftover binding box for finishes.

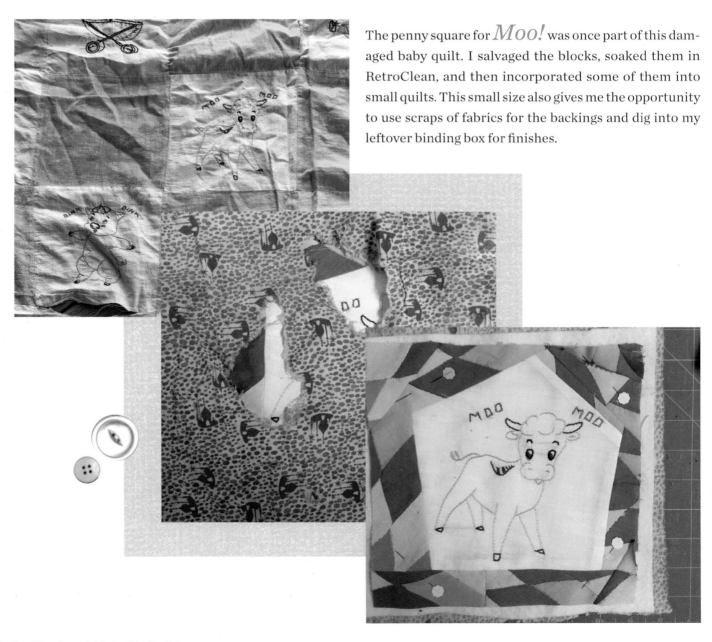

Moo!, 8″ × 8″, machine-quilted by Mary Kerr

The Little Engine That Could and *Bar Fight* were solo blocks that were paired with orphan blocks. Both of these were outline-quilted, and background elements were added. The dense echo quilting in the outer border holds everything in place and allows us to quilt these edges flat.

The Little Engine That Could, 8″ × 8″, machine-quilted by Mary Kerr

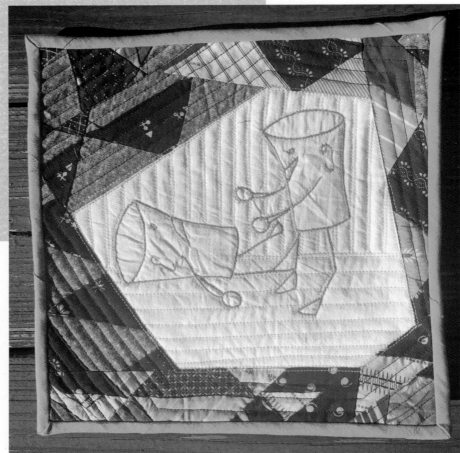

Bar Fight, 9″ × 9″, machine-quilted by Mary Kerr

K Is for Katherine, Karen or Kerr

was an elegant, embroidered block that I paired with a single block from 1890 and the vintage black mourning print that was used in *Alley Cats* (see page 115) and *Shelter in Place* (see page 35).

Sharing the Chores, 12″ × 10″, machine-quilted by Mary Kerr

Sharing the Chores was created using the leftover Mosaic fabrics from *Heart of Our Home* (see page 109). These fragments were added to the salvaged end of a vintage tea towel that celebrates a happy home.

Mending was created using the leftover Mosaic fabrics from *An Apple a Day* (see page 57). This tea towel was once a part of a set of Days of the Week towels from the 1940s. Women were encouraged to focus on one chore each day. I am not sure this lady is thrilled that it is Wednesday.

Cracklin' mats,
4½″ and 6″ square

Mending, 12½″ × 14½″, machine-quilted by Mary Kerr

I Left My Heart in Dixie, 13½″ × 13½″,
machine-quilted by Mary Kerr

I Left My Heart in Dixie features a vintage linen with decorative edging. In order for this trim to be shown, the center part of the top was first pieced in three vertical segments. An extra layer of a coordinating fabric was pinned to the vintage linen just under the decorative edge to complete the length of the outside borders. The sides of this extra fabric were caught in the seams, and the top open edge was hidden by the vintage linen. Last, the top border was added and the decorative edge was tacked down with the quilting stitches. The flannel border fabric for this mini quilt was also used in *Looking West*, on page 98, and *Trade Mark*, on page 103.

Barnyard Breakfast pairs a single embroidered square with vintage blocks from the 1870s. Another vintage block was used for the back. Love this happy little family!

Barnyard Breakfast, 10″ × 11″, machine-quilted by Mary Kerr

Cracklin' mat, 5" × 7½", and
pincushion, 3½" × 3½"

CHAPTER 7

Pillows, Pincushions, and Cracklin' Mats

I have shared small quilts throughout this book that were created with leftover bits and fragments. Sometimes we have stand-alone pieces that are the perfect vehicle for vintage ephemera and special trinkets. Sometimes you have to think outside the box to make these memories shine. Pillows, pincushions, and cracklin' mats are additional options for your make-do creativity.

A cutter quilt is a textile that has been damaged beyond repair. They were overloved and now beg to be made into something that can continue to be cherished and enjoyed. Often these cutter quilts have been purchased in their damaged condition, and other times I am working with fragments that someone else has already cut out of a quilt. The challenge is to decide whether to cut around the damage, cover it with a vintage linen, or embrace the imperfections. Each piece is unique.

I have created pillows with some of the larger pieces. Smaller squares make wonderful pincushions …embellished with buttons, lace, jewelry, hardware, and more. The vintage belt buckle was found in a box of my grandmother's things, and the cheddar, teal, and oxblood fragment complemented the colors perfectly. Now it can be displayed and enjoyed.

Most quilters' least favorite part of creating a pillow is sewing the edges shut so the stitches are hidden. You can solve this dilemma by using an old button-down shirt as the backing. With right sides together, stitch the quilted pillow top and the shirt front on all four sides. Unbutton the shirt front and turn the right sides through the opening. Press well and stitch 1–2 inches from the edge to create a decorative flange. Insert your pillow form and button the shirt placket closed. This is recycling at its finest!

The shirt used on this pillow back was a favorite button-down from my teenage years (yes, my family kept everything!). The extra gingham shirt fabrics were paired with a vintage linen to create *You're Tops*.

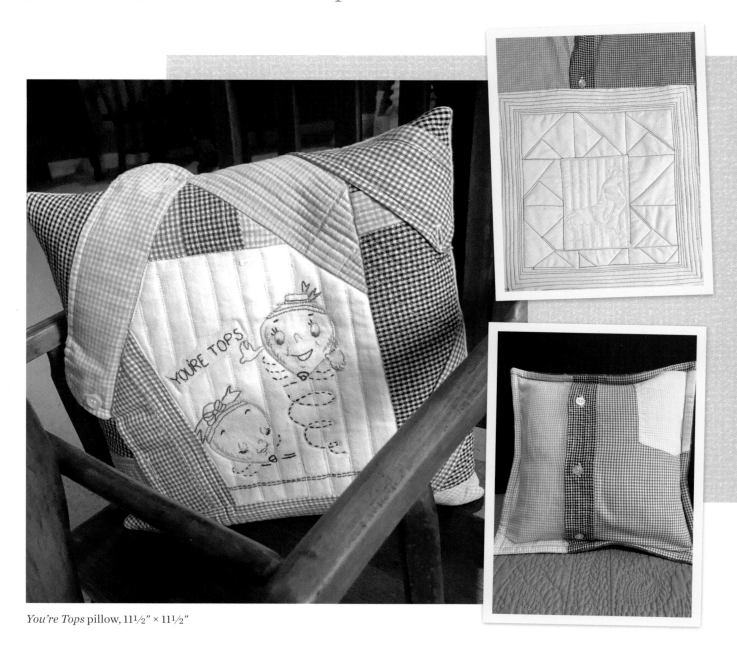

You're Tops pillow, 11½" × 11½"

Ora Coleman (1914–2013) was my great-aunt, and she was rarely seen with without needlework or a crochet hook in her hand. She had no children of her own yet spent many years spoiling nephews and their children. *Remembering Ora* was created when I added one of her doilies to a pillow top and was able to attach one of her vintage belt buckles. The doily was stitched down by machine, and the buckle was secured with hand stitches that went through the pillow to create definition. I tucked a note in the pocket of the shirt on the back so her story can continue to be shared.

Remembering Ora pillow, 10½″ × 10½″

Fusion was created when a very thin Pinwheel block was layered over a top fragment. I first quilted the base and then gently removed the pinwheel unit from its gauzy base. This was then pinned in place and buttonhole was stitched in place. Two quite different blocks that play well together.

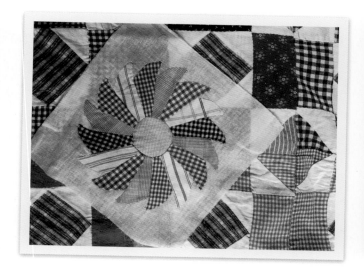

Fusion pillow, 11½″ × 11½″

Sunflower Pillow incorporates fragments left over from *Creamsicles in Chocolate* (see page 42). The vintage base was quilted first, and the petals were then pinned in place. They were secured with machine buttonhole stitches and later embellished with a vintage button.

My friend Dee Datik sent me a stack of block fragments that had been pieced in the 1940s. These unfinished blocks were paired with an adorable Redwork block and made into this cheerful *Dutch Boy* pillow.

Sunflower pillow, 15″ × 15″

Instead of a shirt, I used a scrap of a vintage cutter quilt on the back of this pillow. *Elephant for Ella* was created when I paired a vintage penny square of the elephant Dumbo with fragments of the top used in the *Shot Bag* quilts (see page 104). My youngest granddaughter is wild about elephants, and this worked perfectly as a "Mimi loves me" present!

Starburst Candy pillow, 20″ × 20″, machine-quilted by Dusty Farrell

Starburst Candy Often there are leftover blocks and fabric that beg to be made into something special. I created a coordinating pillow to go with *Fruit Loops* (page 47). I love the opportunity to showcase the very different quilting styles of two equally talented artists, Kelly Cline and Dusty Farrell.

Pincushions are basically tiny pillows that are filled with Poly-fil stuffing, walnut hulls, or a combination of the two. They are a fun way to use up those last scraps from a project.

Cracklin' mats are simply tiny quilts that make my heart sing. These are small memory quilts that can be used as mug rugs and coasters. They can be sent as reminders of loved ones or just an "I love you" gift. Creating these was therapeutic for me, and sometimes that is enough! These cracklin' mats and pincushions can be pieced and quilted in a variety of ways, and some of the variations are shown here. Do not be afraid to use small pieces or new techniques. You do not have a huge expenditure of time or resources on these little projects and can afford to make new design decisions.

PRACTICAL MAKE-DO TOOLBOX

Working with Vintage Fabrics

Some vintage fabrics are in pristine condition, but these are not usually the pieces I choose to work with in my recycling projects. I am drawn to those pieces that have been exposed to a variety of conditions, abuse, and misuse. Ripped seams and frayed edges are common, while other pieces are stained or torn. Many have simply never been completed.

Bear Claw cutter quilt, circa 1880

Sometimes the damage can be repaired, and the quilt top may be finished as originally intended. One can carefully repair the pieces and clean the textile. Edges can be reinforced and separating seams can be resewn. Holes can be patched, and missing fabric replaced.

Dove in the Window blocks, circa 1900

Many orphan textiles suffer from piecing that refuses to lie flat. The multiple piecing and the opportunity for errors combine with bias edges that result in a very wonky textile.

Our current longarm quilting techniques allow us to add enough threadwork so that the top is literally "quilted into submission."

Hint: Plan for distortion if using vintage fragments on the outer edge of your quilt. Once quilting is complete, trim to a straight perfect edge and then bind as desired.

Dirt and Stains

Each of us has our own comfort level when we address the issue of dirt and stains. I see most stains as well-deserved age spots and freckles, but I do prefer to work with clean fabric. If at all possible, I recommend waiting until after the piece is quilted to address stains and discoloration. Any immersion in water will naturally cause some fraying of the seams. If your seam allowance is already scant or raveling, this agitation could cause the seams to separate further. They are far stronger if held in place by quilting stitches.

Having said that, if you are bothered by the condition of your textile, please take the time to wash it before you start playing with it. Most fabrics do well if they are gently handwashed. A gentle soak in a good-quality quilt wash (there are many on the market) will remove surface dirt and some stains. Restoration and Retro Clean are the best products for removing overall yellowing.

Old-fashioned Safeguard soap will remove smoke smells from fabric. Unwrap a bar of white soap, wrap it in a white paper towel, and place the soap and offending textile in a sealed plastic bag for two to three days. Repeat as needed until the odor is removed. The bar of soap can be reused indefinitely.

Wash Day, 14½″ × 12″, machine-quilted by Shannon Shirley

Incorporating Vintage Blocks, Tops, and Fragments

Several of the quilts in this book also feature vintage embroideries, blocks, and tops that have been recycled from unfinished or damaged textiles. These vintage blocks are not for the perfectionist quilter, since they were often left undone for good reason. They are perfect for the make-do quilter! I personally love the challenge, and I encourage you to breathe new life into these imperfect pieces. Many blocks were not finished because of inferior workmanship. Check the seam allowances to ensure that the pieces will not separate as they are pressed and sewn into a new project. If there is not a quarter inch around the outside of the design, you may lose points and the overall image will be distorted. A number of the blocks we work with are not square, and they vary in size. Some of us are not bothered by these issues, and others prefer to remake the offending designs. The choice is up to you!

Poor-quality fabrics can distort the quilt pieces, causing the blocks to stretch or pull out of shape. Thin fabrics can be reinforced with interfacing or another layer of cotton.

TIPS TO REMEMBER

❏ Vintage and contemporary fabrics mix well

❏ It is okay to combine vintage fabrics from
   multiple eras

❏ Embellishments can be used to cover a multitude
   of flaws

❏ Any textile can be incorporated into
   a new quilt

❏ Ignore the quilt police—they are not invited to
   your party

❏ Give yourself permission to play and
   Make Do

❏ Think outside your normal box

❏ Document your story

❏ Relax, enjoy, and create what makes your
   heart sing!

FUN ON THE BACKSIDE

The back of your quilt is the perfect place to add additional memory pieces that may not fit or be exciting enough to use on the front of the quilt. In the "Feed Sack Frenzy" chapter, I shared a number of pieces that incorporated vintage feed sacks as the backings. These tend to be heavier, dense fabrics that would be difficult to hand-quilt. They are perfect for machine quilting and longarming. Play with a practice piece first to see if needle size or tension needs to be adjusted for your specific machine.

See quilt on page 87.

See quilt on page 116.

I love using vintage fabrics on the backs of my quilt. These can be yard goods, as seen in *Creamsicles in Chocolate* and *Alley Cats*. *Mother and Child* used a vintage tablecloth as its back. As a make-do quilter, you can make any fabric work.

Pathways (see page 36), *Bicycle Built for Two* (see page 67), and *Chicken Basket* (see page 49) all used a simple vintage top for the back. You will need to work around multiple seams while quilting, but the final effect is well worth it. The back for *Four Square* (see page 39) was pieced with the leftover blocks. There are no rules!

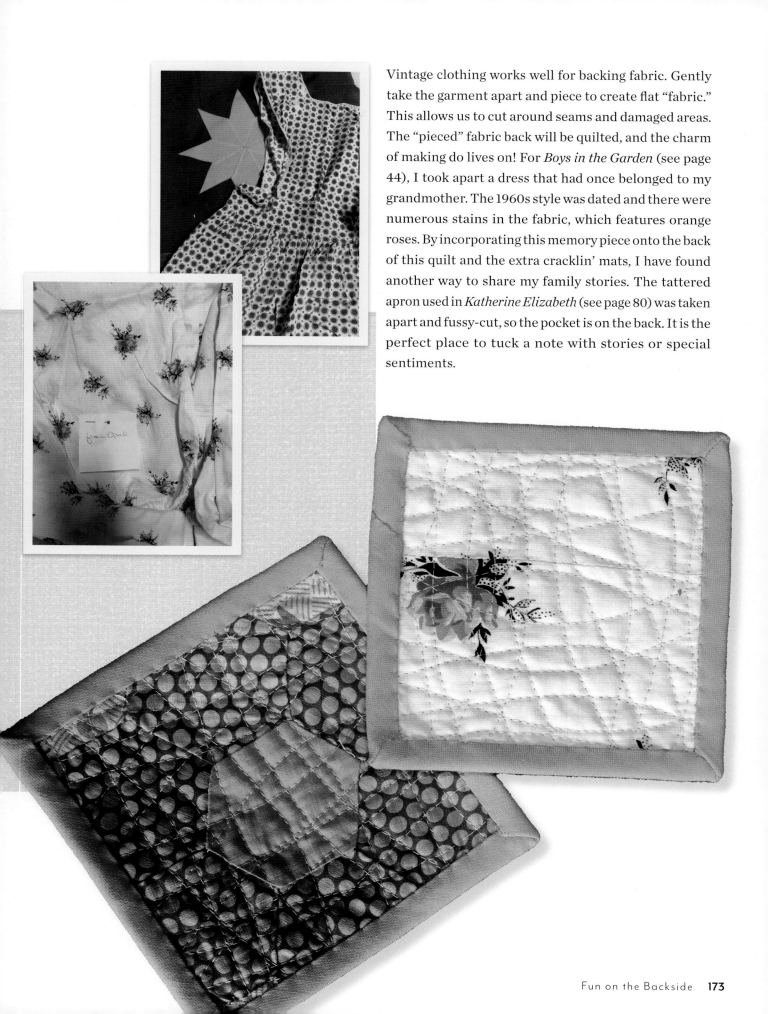

Vintage clothing works well for backing fabric. Gently take the garment apart and piece to create flat "fabric." This allows us to cut around seams and damaged areas. The "pieced" fabric back will be quilted, and the charm of making do lives on! For *Boys in the Garden* (see page 44), I took apart a dress that had once belonged to my grandmother. The 1960s style was dated and there were numerous stains in the fabric, which features orange roses. By incorporating this memory piece onto the back of this quilt and the extra cracklin' mats, I have found another way to share my family stories. The tattered apron used in *Katherine Elizabeth* (see page 80) was taken apart and fussy-cut, so the pocket is on the back. It is the perfect place to tuck a note with stories or special sentiments.

I am a huge fan of memory pieces and have been blessed with lots of family linens, works in progress, oddities, fabric stashes, and more. One piece that came from my aunt Nellie Horne (1918–2012) was a simple linen towel that had been patched. Make-do at its finest, and I was proud to include it on the back of *Mary's Garden* (see page 55). What pieces do you have that can be incorporated into your make-do design?

THE DESIGN PROCESS

I design by the project and add additional elements as I go. I choose my focus and build from there. This could be a special block, a specific embroidered linen, a cherished piece of jewelry, a funky block . . . the possibilities are endless. I start pulling additional fabrics and blocks that might play well together, and see what happens. I lay them out together and take pictures of the grouping. Sometimes I change my mind a dozen times until I get something that makes my heart sing. Part of the magic of making do is working with what you have. I often make what I call "seed bags" . . . a clear ziplock bag of items I think will play well together. I allow them to marinate, and I add to the bag as new elements are found.

Allow yourself to change your designs in progress if something does not seem right. Photograph your piece and play with the crop features on your phone. What would it look like if I did this? Both *Horace the Horse* (see page 121) and *Murphy's Barnyard* (see page 97) were cut down when the border I chose was not the right proportion.

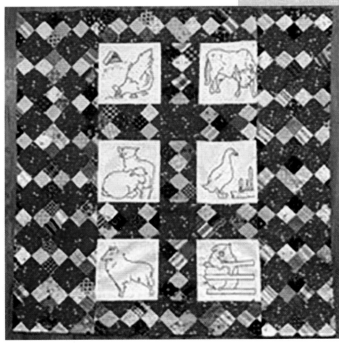

My initial plan for *Temperance* (see below and page 132) was to use a fragment of this vintage T-top. The neutral blocks were overwhelming, so I took them out to create a green border of half-block units.

My vintage chicken embroidery block was overwhelmed by the bold-red piecing in this top. The colors worked but the scale was wrong in my mind. I took pictures as I removed borders until it just felt right. What was originally intended to be a wall hanging is now a very happy pillow.

I loved the initial combination of this embroidered tea towel and the vintage indigo blocks. When it was set together as a small memory quilt, I was not a fan of the "china" lettering. I wanted to showcase the teacups and floral embroidery, so this was remade into five smaller pieces . . . a small quilt and four festive pincushions. Creating these smaller pieces is a great way to share a single memory piece with multiple family members.

Elements were carefully removed from the outer border of *Orange Is a Neutral* (see page 41) to create a less choppy flow.

See *Hummingbird Kisses* on page 71.

See *Barnyard Breakfast* on page 152.

See *Alley Cats* on page 135.

LABELS AND DOCUMENTATION

As contemporary quilters, we have been told over and over that each of our quilts needs to be labeled. At minimum, we are instructed to provide the maker's name, the quilter's name, and the date the quilt was created. There are a number of ways to create these labels, and they range from the very basic to elaborately embellished story cards.

When we are working with vintage pieces, I feel we have an obligation to provide as much information as possible. I encourage my students to document all that they know about the textile, and to establish a connection to their intended recipient. Include circa dates for your fabrics, and document what you used to create your quilt.

I have frequently created labels by using vintage blocks. I apply a fusible web to the back and write the information directly on the block, using fabric pens. I list the maker of the vintage linen, when I created the piece, who quilted it, and why I was inspired to make this particular quilt. The labels shown here are found on the backs of quilts in this book.

Another wonderful option is to use photo transfer software to incorporate a picture of the maker or recipient (or both) into your label. A vintage photo can be scanned into your computer, and supporting details can be added and printed out onto photo transfer paper. I frame this label with strips of fabric and appliqué it to the back of the quilt. This technique allows us to perpetuate our cherished memories and pass them on to future generations.

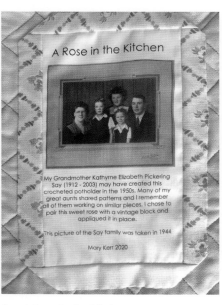

See *The House on Claret Mountain* on page 61.

See *A Rose in the Kitchen* on page 114.

See *Blue Flowers for Karen* on page 56.

VARIATIONS IN QUILTING

The quilting stitches are the glue that holds a quilt together. These decorative stitches add definition, dimension, and another layer of design to a textile. How to finish a quilt is an age-old dilemma, and many of us struggle with these decisions. Fortunately, there are as many different ways to finish a quilt as there are quilters who work on them. Each individual brings their own talents and tastes to the worktable.

To share my process, I have quilted many of the smaller pieces in this book on my domestic machine. My machine quilting is quite simple . . . outline stitches, straight lines, and simple waves. I feel that the simplicity of my quilting allows these smaller pieces to shine. I do not drop my feeds, I move slowly, and I celebrate the process. All of the quilts and my quilting were done on an extremely basic Bernina 135. This works perfectly with my own "make it work" mentality.

I have chosen to have most of the larger quilts in this book finished by others. I love the collaborative magic that happens when I work with a variety of artists to showcase these make-do pieces. The name of each quilter is listed prominently on my quilt label, and I believe that they should be credited in any and all exhibition paperwork. I was thrilled to collaborate with each of these talented artists. My work would not have been the same without the addition of their support, encouragement, and artistry.

Diana Reinhart Annis
Norton, Massachusetts
Institchesquilts@aol.com

Diana Beverage
Marlinton, West Virginia

Doris Bloomer
Appling, Georgia
dbl1960@yahoo.com

Kelly Cline
Lawrence, Kansas
www.kellyclinequilting.com

Jill Coleman
Biglerville, Pennsylvania
aquilter16@hotmail.com

Barbara Dann
Bellefonte, Pennsylvania
www.alleycatquiltworks.com

Dusty Farrell
Guys Mills, Pennsylvania
www.farrellscountrystitchin.com

Jane Hauprich
Centerville, Maryland
www.stitchbystitchcustomquilting.com

Lucinda Herring
Pinckney, Michigan
https://quiltsbylucinda.home.blog

Debbie Kauffman
Minot, North Dakota
www.DSRdesignsquilts.com

Vicki Maloney
Fredericksburg, Virginia
jvmaloney@gmail.com

Cheryl Morgan
Broad Run, Virginia
mmquilting@gmail.com

Quilting detail from *Orange Is a Neutral* (see page 41), machine-quilted by Jane Hauprich

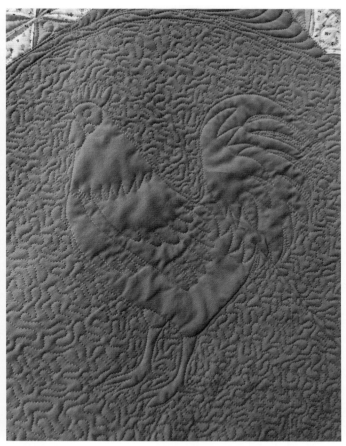

Quilting detail from *Baskets of Chicken* (see page 49), quilted by Kris Vierra

Lynn O'Neal
Seabrook, South Carolina
creativeclutter2010@yahoo.com

Deb Peterson
Chippewa Falls, Wisconsin
Petersdk@uwec.edu

Michael and MaryGin Rettman
Bel Air, Maryland
www.froggywentapainting.weebly.com

Januari Rhodes
King George, Virginia
www.thequiltedginger.com

Shannon Shirley
Woodbridge, Virginia
www.onceinarabbitmoon.com

Mo Starkey
King George, Virginia
www.materialnotions.com

Connie Stover
Morenci, Michigan
www.quilting-by-connie.wixsite.com

Marcia Swanson
Omaha, Nebraska
www.dogearcreekquilts.com

Kris Vierra
Kansas City, Missouri
www.quilterontherun.com

Allison Wilbur
Barrington, Rhode Island
www.allisonwilburquilts.com

EPILOGUE

In celebration of our make-do attitudes, I encourage you to use those unexpected and unique pieces . . . blocks, feed sacks, clothing, ephemera, and more. Create a new piece that honors the quilters who came before, while adding your own unique style and aesthetic. Give yourself permission to complete it in a new and exciting way. By incorporating fragments and memory pieces into a contemporary quilt, new life is breathed into the textile, allowing it to continue to be appreciated, enjoyed, and, yes, remembered.

Thank you for allowing me to share my love of make-do quilting! I look forward to seeing what you create, celebrate, and share.

ACKNOWLEDGMENTS

Thank you to my editor, Sandra Korinchak, and the staff at Schiffer Publishing, Ltd., for their unending encouragement and support. Thank you to my husband, Ralph, for his patient support and his help with photography. Thank you to my sister, Karen Mitchell, for reading the manuscript in progress and helping to organize my thoughts. And last but not least, thank you to my family and to the women in my life who serve as my army of cheerleaders. Life would not be the same without you!

INDEX